MW01119655

STATIONS OF THE CROSS
FOR PERSONS
WITH DISABILITIES

Msgr. Thomas McDonnell

Our Sunday Visitor Publishing Division
Our Sunday Visitor, Inc.
Huntington, Indiana 46750

Nihil Obstat: Fr. Michael Heintz, Censor Librorum
Imprimatur: ✠ John M. D'Arcy
Bishop of Fort Wayne-South Bend
September 21, 2006

The *Nihil Obstat* and *Imprimatur* are official declarations that a book or pamphlet is free of doctrinal or moral error. No implication is contained therein that those who have granted the *Nihil Obstat* or *Imprimatur* agree with the contents, opinions, or statements expressed.

The Scripture citations used in this work are taken from the *Catholic Edition of the Revised Standard Version of the Bible* (RSV), copyright © 1965 and 1966 by the Division of Christian Education of the National Council of the Churches of Christ in the United States of America. Used by permission. All rights reserved.

Every reasonable effort has been made to determine copyright holders of excerpted materials and to secure permissions as needed. If any copyrighted materials have been inadvertently used in this work without proper credit being given in one form or another, please notify Our Sunday Visitor in writing so that future printings of this work may be corrected accordingly.

Copyright © 2006 by Our Sunday Visitor Publishing Division, Our Sunday Visitor, Inc. Published 2006

11 10 09 08 07 06   1 2 3 4 5 6 7 8 9

All rights reserved. With the exception of short excerpts for critical reviews, no part of this work may be reproduced or transmitted in any form or by any means whatsoever without permission in writing from the publisher. Write:

Our Sunday Visitor Publishing Division
Our Sunday Visitor, Inc.
200 Noll Plaza
Huntington, IN 46750

ISBN: 978-1-59276-287-3 (Inventory No. T377)
LCCN: 2006931319

Cover design by Rebecca J. Heaston
Interior design by Sherri L. Hoffman
Interior art: The Crosiers
Special thanks to Sr. Michelle Grgurich, VSC
Director, Catholic Department for Persons with Disabilities
Secretariat for Education of the Diocese of Pittsburgh
for her thoughtful input and assistance.

PRINTED IN CHINA

INTRODUCTION

It was St. Bonaventure who reminded us that there is another approach to deepening one's relationship with Christ than our usual, traditional approach. His would be an emphasis on leading us to see with "the eyes of your hearts" (Eph. 1:18). Thus in his *The Journey of the Mind to God*, he wrote:

> *If you ask how such things can occur, seek the answer in God's grace, not in doctrine; in the longings of the will, not in understanding; in the insights of prayer, not in research; seek the bridegroom, not the teacher.*

This approach of finding "solutions" in a relationship with Christ the Bridegroom is an often neglected part of our theological, catechetical, and even pastoral approach.

Admitting the shallowness of language, we have nevertheless become aware, more than ever, of the needs of all of us who live every day with disabilities . . . and solutions that can meet those needs. Among the best solutions we find, of course, is prayer.

Prayer — forming a closer bond with our Lord — will help us counteract the prevailing utilitarian atmosphere in our culture, one which undermines a person's self-image and sense of worth. We are all "disabled" in some way, merely by being human and imperfect. Thus, every person has a contribution to make to our Church and to our society:

> *So we do not lose heart. Though our outer nature is wasting away, our inner nature is being renewed every day. For this slight momentary affliction is preparing us for an eternal weight of glory beyond all comparison.*
> — 2 Cor. 4:16-17

More than 25 years of ministering with persons with disabilities has taught me the role that the power of affirmation plays in everyone's life. This is the conclusion from secular sources (*The Miracle Worker* — the story of Anne Sullivan and Helen Keller) as well as spiritual writings (the journals of Raissia Maritan). I hope that the following reflections upon the Stations of the Cross, in the context and life of persons with disabilities, may prove to be a source of affirmation — and also a source of help for individuals to develop their full potential.

The Psalmist once wrote, "In thy (God's) light, do we see light" (Ps. 36:9). It is in our relationship with the divine that we see ourselves and our vocations in proper perspective. In my opinion, this is especially true for people with disabilities, growing in relationship with the divine through their relationship to the crucified Lord.

FIRST STATION

Jesus Is Condemned to Death

V. We adore you, O Christ, and we bless you,
R. Because by your holy Cross, you have redeemed the world.

"Then he (Pilate) handed him over to them to be crucified" (Jn. 19:16).

No matter how the scene is depicted artistically, at this moment, Jesus is psychically standing alone. Throughout the Gospel, he maintained a deep consciousness of intimacy with the Father (e.g. Jn. 16:32). But — perhaps because of the immediacy of his pain — at this moment, he anticipates the cry from the cross: "My God, my God, why hast thou forsaken me?" (Mk.15:34). Pain can have that effect.

Sometimes being in pain, even simply the pain of loneliness, can obscure Christ's personalized promise given at Baptism: "I am with you always, to the close of the age" (Mt. 28:20). But if I see with the eyes of the heart, I am able to focus on this moment as a grace.

Jesus, your aloneness was an aloneness suffered for others, and this is the same redemptive opportunity that I've been offered. When I feel that I am standing alone, I can gaze upward and remember that I am united with you. I can pray for understanding and reach out in prayer for others.

RESOLUTION: We pray for all people who are isolated or feel alone, that they will know that they stand with Christ.

Our Father, Hail Mary, Glory Be

SECOND STATION

Jesus Receives His Cross

V. We adore you, O Christ, and we bless you,
R. Because by your holy Cross, you have redeemed the world.

Lord, all our lives we struggle with the puzzle of why suffering exists. This must also have been the question which tore at your heart like a fishhook: *why?*

It is a question I often ask, especially when I am feeling discouraged. Upon reflection, I realize that this was part of your high priestly act — and I console myself with the fact that "we have not a high priest who is unable to sympathize with our weaknesses" (Heb. 4:15). When I think about this, I realize that you understand my feelings and experiences.

I trust that since I share in your Cross, *you will give me rest as you promise.* Although the frustration may remain, by identifying with you, I will gain spiritual strength to endure and grow.

Nor is my disability fruitless; it is a grace. And I pray that I may make Paul's words my own: "Now I rejoice in my sufferings for your sake, and in my flesh I complete what is lacking in Christ's afflictions for the sake of his body, that is, the church" (Col. 1:24).

RESOLUTION: We beg for the grace to understand the role our disabilities play in God's redemptive plan.

Our Father, Hail Mary, Glory Be

THIRD STATION

Jesus Falls the First Time

V. We adore you, O Christ, and we bless you,
R. Because by your holy Cross, you have redeemed the world.

As I ponder this station, many thoughts rush into my mind. Instinctively, I realize how I often fall far short of my goals. I realize the truth of St. Paul's words: "I do not understand my own actions. For I do not what I want, but I do the very thing I hate . . . I do not do the good that I want, but the evil I do not want is what I do" (Rom. 7:15-19). I identify with the words of Teilhard de Chardin's sister Marguerite, who, in her own struggles with illness, wrote:

> Lord, the journey comes to a close, giving me, as others, the impression of complete failure. I've done nothing for you: no conscious prayer. . . . I haven't ever conquered these childlike tempers. . . . (And) in vain, I promise to do better.

Because you once fell, Jesus, I know that you understand.

In the millisecond after you stumbled and before you crashed to earth, your own human nature must have questioned how much more pain the Father would demand of you. As you lay on the ground, struggling to get up, you must have repeated the constant prayer, "Your will be done." May your words become mine.

RESOLUTION: We pray to accept God's will in our lives.

Our Father, Hail Mary, Glory Be

FOURTH STATION

Jesus Meets His Mother

V. We adore you, O Christ, and we bless you,
R. Because by your holy Cross, You have redeemed the world.

Helplessness — on so many levels — is a part of the disability scene. We might think of countless mothers and fathers who give birth to a child with disabilities. We can see and feel their utter helplessness. Though children may be unaware of it, much about our culture is hostile and challenges their very right to be born — beginning, of course, with the subtle and not-so-subtle pressure from doctors and others on their parents to terminate such pregnancies.

Some of us find ourselves unable to perform basic human functions, i.e., bathing and dressing ourselves, eating, or communicating. In a society that emphasizes an individual's "usefulness," this can be devastating to our self-image.

As I reflect upon the Fourth Station, however, I find myself immersed in the mystery of redemptive helplessness. Because of the distance and the crowd, Jesus, you and your mother could not speak to each other. You were prevented from instinctively reaching out to embrace each other — that type of touch that brings consolation. It's doubtful that you could even communicate with your eyes; yours were so swollen and disfigured due to the beating you received, and Mary's vision was blurred by her tears.

Of old, the Psalmist cried, "I suffer thy terrors; I am helpless" (Ps. 88:15). Such was his desolation. This must have been what you and your mother were feeling at that moment. And, because you have experienced such helplessness, I can come to you, knowing you will understand and support me.

RESOLUTION: We pray for the grace to realize that our helplessness is often a part of the contemporary cross.

Our Father, Hail Mary, Glory Be

FIFTH STATION

Simon of Cyrene Helps Jesus Carry His Cross

V. We adore you, O Christ, and we bless you,
R. Because by your holy Cross, you have redeemed the world.

Simon, like most disciples, began as a learner. Then, he became a teacher whose message can speak to all of us.

Initially, Simon was "enlisted" or "compelled" into service (Mk. 15:21). Obviously, he did not recognize who you were, Lord, and the grace being offered to him. His insensitivity is a call to all of us in the Church community to take your words "as you did it to one of the least of these my brethren, you did it to me" (Mt. 25) seriously and literally. Encountering anyone in need offers me the opportunity to touch Christ.

Jesus, you had twelve legions of angels at your disposal. But in God's providence, Simon was chosen to help instead. In allowing Simon to carry your Cross, you showed that no one is meant to carry his or her cross alone without human support. For those of us being ministered to, this contains a message of openness and patience; for those ministering, the message is a reminder to develop a deeper consciousness of the needs of all people.

As I consider Simon's initial reluctance, I realize that God often makes us — as he did Simon — saints in spite of ourselves. When by "practical" standards I am weak, dealing with loneliness (and sometimes anger and rebellion), this is a consoling truth.

RESOLUTION: We pray for the Church, that it may realize its call to help us to cultivate our spiritual lives.

Our Father, Hail Mary, Glory Be

SIXTH STATION

Veronica Wipes the Face of Jesus

V. We adore you, O Christ, and we bless you,
R. Because by your holy Cross, you have redeemed the world.

Amazingly enough, there is no biblical foundation for this station — yet the Christian community has included Veronica in the Passion story handed on from the earliest centuries. Even today, in St. Peter's Basilica, there is a prominent statue of Veronica holding a veil with the face of the Lord delicately etched upon it.

While I can draw many lessons from her story — e.g., the force of her spirituality, her instinct, her courage — right now, I spend a moment contemplating her name. The word *Veronica* translates as a "true" image or icon — in this case, an icon of Christ. Thus, even her name can remind me of a myriad of truths.

Through Baptism, Jesus, your face has been imprinted in our souls in such a way that every time the Father looks down upon us, he sees your face and is compelled to love us. In this sense, then, we are all "true icons" in your image.

St. Thérèse of Lisieux, the "Little Flower," reminds me that through suffering, I am more and more conformed to Christ; only in heaven will any of us be able to truly appreciate the resemblance. But suffice to say that our disabilities lead us more and more to resemble the crucified Christ. This is the key to the power of my prayer life and my intercession for others.

RESOLUTION: We pray for the grace to understand that we are true images of Christ.

Our Father, Hail Mary, Glory Be

SEVENTH STATION

Jesus Falls a Second Time

V. We adore you, O Christ, and we bless you,
R. Because by your holy Cross, you have redeemed the world.

Teilhard de Chardin once remarked, "The road along which his kingdom makes progress is the way of relinquishment, of blood and tears — the way of the cross." Reading these words and accepting them in faith is relatively easy. But living them is difficult, very difficult.

As I ponder this station, it shouts to me of pain, weakness, and confusion. It is obvious, Jesus, that it was weakness that caused you to fall again. Your strength was draining away. On purely human terms, your body was probably crying out for a few seconds of unconsciousness — a merciful darkness which would shroud both senses and reason.

Lord, when weakness eats away at me on every level, even at my spiritual strivings, help me to remember the words of St. Francis de Sales: "(Perfection) is never finished. We must always begin again, and begin again willingly."

"When a man has finished," says Scripture, "he is just beginning" (Sir. 18:7). What we have done up to the present is good, but what we shall begin will be even better. When I find verbal prayer difficult, give me the grace to form the intention that my body itself become a prayer — my own "host" by which I worship the Father.

RESOLUTION: We pray for the grace to overcome the temptation of discouragement.

Our Father, Hail Mary, Glory Be

EIGHTH STATION

Jesus Meets the Women of Jerusalem

V. We adore you, O Christ, and we bless you,
R. Because by your holy Cross, you have redeemed the world.

We tend to think that the Giver of All Gifts is self-sufficient, in need of nothing. Yet this station points to the opposite truth: namely, that Christ the Giver is also Christ the Receiver. At this moment in time, Jesus, you were alone, hurting, and rejected. In a very real way, you needed support and consolation. You found it in the women of Jerusalem and their empathetic tears.

If I can believe the words you spoke to St. Margaret Mary, even in our time you remain a Man in need:

> *Behold the heart which has loved men so much that it has spared nothing, even to exhausting and consuming itself, to prove its love to them. And as thanks, I receive from the greater number only ingratitude . . .*

In this light, part of my vocation is to express my gratitude to you as Lord by giving you my love — and accepting my calling to the Cross.

The medieval mystic Meister Eckhart maintained that the word "woman" is the noblest word one can address to the soul — stressing the areas of openness and fruitfulness. Thus, the presence of women at this station has a symbolic importance attached. They remind me to be open to the words of Christ ("If anyone wishes to follow me, he/she must take up the cross") and to pray that the presence of the Cross in my life may prove to be fruitful, both for my own sake and that of the Church.

RESOLUTION: We pray for a greater appreciation of Christ's love for ourselves, the Church, and the world.

Our Father, Hail Mary, Glory Be

NINTH STATION

Jesus Falls a Third Time

V. We adore you, O Christ, and we bless you,
R. Because by your holy Cross, you have redeemed the world.

Lord, you knew what was in store for you. You had prophesied in the Garden of Gethsemane, "This is your hour, and the power of darkness" (Lk. 22:53). Perhaps it was to emphasize the very "power" of darkness that an unwritten tradition has us focus on the third fall. Seeing how all your wounds were torn open again, we glimpse its force. But I believe there is more to see here as well.

First, we might ask, where was Simon of Cyrene? After his earlier appearance, suddenly he is absent in depictions of this station. Perhaps Simon lacked the strength and desire — at this stage — to bear the Cross. Maybe he did not perceive the redemptive role he was asked to play. After a long period of time, I can begin to feel the same way.

There is what we might term a "negative spiritual gravity," which constantly tries to pull us from our Christian vision to a more prosaic, horizontal approach. It is often the cause of our becoming discouraged.

Again, Jesus, I think of the force of gravity pulling you so painfully to the earth. Such a fall no doubt took your breath away. But herein lies a redemptive paradox. Now the Spirit — the *ruah* or "breath" of God — fills your being and propels you forward. And if I ask for the Spirit's help, especially in my moments of discouragement, he will also fill my being.

RESOLUTION: We pray that the Spirit of God will lift us up in our moments of discouragement.

Our Father, Hail Mary, Glory Be

TENTH STATION

Jesus Is Stripped of His Garments

V. We adore you, O Christ, and we bless you,
R. Because by your holy Cross, you have redeemed the world.

This is a station I can identify with. It can feel like an invasion of privacy at times when I need someone to assist me. Human beings do not like to expose their truest selves.

As you were being stripped, Lord, perhaps you had similar feelings regarding the invasion of your privacy. But in this case, there was also a deeper spiritual symbolism, tracing its roots to the story of Adam and Eve. When they had sinned, their first reaction was to clothe themselves, as if hiding from God. Note how God addressed a question to Adam: "Where are you?" (Gen. 3:9). God is constantly asking this same question of us: Where are we in our relationship with Him? Do we truly try to cultivate His friendship?

You, the Sinless One, could appear shamelessly naked before God. This truth thus reminds me that I need to approach God exactly as I am. So often, Lord, I can be tempted to present an edited version of myself when I come to you in prayer. But actually, exactly the opposite is the case: you tell us that we need not try to cover up or hide our weaknesses and ambiguities.

RESOLUTION: We learn from the Psalmist, who cried, "In thy light do we see light" (Ps. 36:9). We pray for the insight to look at ourselves as God does — seeing our faults and failings, but also our potentials.

Our Father, Hail Mary, Glory Be

ELEVENTH STATION

Jesus Is Nailed to the Cross

V. We adore you, O Christ, and we bless you,
R. Because by your holy Cross, you have redeemed the world.

Sometimes, Lord, our hands or feet just don't want to perform so many functions. Some of us cannot walk, or cannot feed ourselves. And on those occasions when we attend Mass, some of us can offer the sign of peace only with our eyes.

On the other hand, Jesus, I can see deep symbolism attached to this station. Your arms are being stretched beyond their human capacity. They are pulled out of their sockets — reminding us of your redemptive desire and ever-growing capacity to embrace more and more people in your love.

Indeed, the "eyes of the heart," which St. Paul encourages us to cultivate, lead me to see a redemptive paradox: while your hands and feet are rendered powerless, I can glimpse an integral part of the redemptive dynamic in which you reach out to, and redeem, the whole world.

A French mystic, Paul Claudel, once put forth the idea that "dependency" was a prime characteristic of God and of Christ. By this, he meant that the work of God and of Christ now depends (in the widest sense) upon us. "But grace was given to each of us according to the measure of Christ's gift" (Eph. 4:7). By the acceptance of our crosses, especially the cross of helplessness, we become instruments for bringing Christ's redeeming love into our world.

RESOLUTION: We pray that by patiently accepting our limits, we will encourage others to be stretched beyond their human capacity to respond with compassion.

Our Father, Hail Mary, Glory Be

TWELFTH STATION

Jesus Dies on the Cross

V. We adore you, O Christ, and we bless you,
R. Because by your holy Cross, you have redeemed the world.

Our hearts are agitated until someone truly understands us; this is a basic truth. Perhaps, Lord, this lack of understanding from the majority of onlookers was your deepest pain on Calvary. Sometimes, we can feel that those around us do not understand our struggles; frequently, we struggle even to find some self-understanding and meaning in our own experience of disability. Perhaps the Father's words to St. Catherine of Siena can help us to "see" the meaning in our difficulties:

> . . . it is by means of my servants and their great suffering that I would be merciful to the world and reform my bride the Church.

And again:

> Truly these last can be called another Christ crucified, my only-begotten Son. . . . (they) become mediators in prayer, in word, in good holy living, setting themselves up as examples to others. The precious stones of virtue shine in patience as they bear other's sins.

In writing these thoughts, I can claim only a beginner's insight. But as I read and reread the Gospel accounts of the Passion, one thing I find intriguing is the difference in the attitudes of the two thieves. One taunts you; the other seeks solace in you. The difference, it seems to me, is that the former concentrated on self and his suffering, while the "good" thief concentrated on you. As long as we gaze upon you and identify with you on the Cross, we will find strength and consolation.

RESOLUTION: We pray for the grace to see the meaning of the Cross, and our crosses, through Christ's eyes.

Our Father, Hail Mary, Glory Be

THIRTEENTH STATION

Jesus Is Taken Down from the Cross

V. We adore you, O Christ, and we bless you,
R. Because by your holy Cross, you have redeemed the world.

When we gaze upon this scene, immortalized by Michelangelo's *Pietà*, we wish statues could talk. We see the lifeless (but, paradoxically, life-giving) body of Christ, lying in his mother's arms. No tears are present; she's already cried as many tears as one human being can. And I wonder what Mary's thoughts were at this moment.

Francis Thompson, with a poet's sensitivity, tried to capture the feelings of the moment in his poem "The Passion of Mary":

The soldiers struck a triple stoke,
That smote thy Jesus on the tree;
He broke the Heart of Hearts, as broke
The saint's and Mother's heart in thee.
Thy Son went up the angels' way,
His passion ended; but, ah me!
Thou found'st the road of further days,
A longer way of Calvary.

In the poet's mind, Mary's Passion was longer, since it continued after that nightmare experience on Calvary. And because Christ gave us Mary as our Mother, she still reaches out to comfort and console those who are now suffering with and in Christ. As my Mother — as well as Comforter of the Afflicted — she knows my needs, hurts, and wants. Thus, I can turn to her as Our Lady of Consolation and ask for her help.

RESOLUTION: We pray for the grace to realize that Mary is intimately concerned with us and, as our Mother, feels our pain.

Our Father, Hail Mary, Glory Be

FOURTEENTH STATION

Jesus Is Laid in the Tomb

V. We adore you, O Christ, and we bless you,
R. Because by your holy Cross, you have redeemed the world.

Very little attention is paid to Joseph of Arimathea, perhaps because he appears so late in the Gospel. But he did care for your disfigured earthly Body, Lord, as he took you from the Cross and laid you in a new tomb. The Gospel of John emphasizes this point in a subtle way: with your death, a "new creation" began.

As I reflect upon Joseph of Arimathea, I see him as a model disciple for our time — especially as we attempt to infuse the Church with a vital redemptive energy through acceptance of our crosses. Especially during these trying times, we should never lose faith in the Church.

In his work, *Suffering*, Louis Everly points out that, at times, the Church will become a cross for the believer. If certain parties in the Church show us insensitivity or indifference, we have then experienced the Church as a cross. Let us, then, reflect upon his words:

> *The Church is not the invention of man but of God. If she wholly satisfied us, she would be untrue, for she would be ours. Happy is the man for whom the Church is the cross. He is sure to end up with God. If the Church is mysterious, disappointing, excruciating, it is because God is at work in her. Those who expect a Church which succeeds where God has "failed" believe neither in God nor in the Church.*

If the Church has been a cross for us, let us join our feelings with the Cross of Christ.

RESOLUTION: We pray that our past hurts and anger toward the Church may be transformed into energy for building up the Church.

Our Father, Hail Mary, Glory Be

WORDS OF AFFIRMATION
from Popes John Paul II and Paul VI

Thank you for the suffering you bear in your bodies and your hearts. Thank you for your example of acceptance and of union with the suffering Christ. Thank you for filling up "what is lacking in the suffering of Christ for the sake of his Body, the Church" (Col. 1:24).

— Pope John Paul II

We offer you the truth that alone responds to the mystery of suffering and affords . . . a solace that is without illusions. That truth demands faith in our identity with the Man of Sorrows . . . crucified for our sins and our salvation . . . You are the aristocracy of the Kingdom of God . . . . And if but choose to do so, you work out with Him the world's salvation. This is the Christian understanding of suffering; it is the only one that puts your hearts at rest.

— Pope Paul VI